# Release a Rag

## The Bread & Roses Poetry Award Anthology 2019

### Edited by Mike Quille

### with a Foreword by Alan Morrison

*This is no world for poets, particularly poor ones, to live in*

— Alexander Bethune, labourer and poet
(1804–1843)

First published 2019 by **Culture Matters**.
**Culture Matters** promotes a socialist and progressive approach to art, culture and politics. We run a website which publishes creative and critical material on politics and culture; manage Bread and Roses arts awards; deliver cultural education workshops to trade unionists; publish books; and contribute to the development of culture policy in the labour movement.
See www.culturematters.org.uk

Copyright © the contributors
Cover image © Martin Rowson
ISBN 978-1-912710-21-8

**Acknowledgements**

Thanks to Unite the Union, and in particular their Director of Education, Jim Mowatt, for supporting this Award.

# Foreword: *Precariat Poetry*

By Alan Morrison,
Associate Editor, Culture Matters

*'This is no world for poets, particularly poor ones, to live in'* opined Fifeshire day-labourer-cum-poet, Alexander Bethune (1804–1843), in spite of belated literary success, two centuries ago. Sadly this sentiment still applies to many in the early twenty-first century, where perennially impecunious poets find themselves in the ranks of the ever-swelling contemporary 'Precariat'.

There are many socially disadvantaged poets writing today who could so easily employ that Bethune epithet for their own lots. They miraculously manage to write poems in spite of poverty, whether in work or out of it, on benefits, or zero-hours contracts, and in many respects, too, precisely because of their material poverty. They see poetry as a spiritual response to brutal material diminishment; poetry as a political act in response to the depersonalisation and disempowerment of often imposed and poorly paid employment; poetry as a psychical protection from impersonal forces of consumerism; poetry as protest against perceived societal injustices; and poetry as a paper weapon and vision of a better world.

What we are essentially pinpointing here is socialist poetry. By that I mean poetry which is independent from —and in some instances, openly opposed to— dominant contemporary postmodernist poetry and poetics that are implicitly apolitical, polemically complacent, and overly preoccupied with ironic poses (a type of bourgeois, trustified literary product which Christopher Caudwell disparaged as 'capitalist poetry' in *Illusion and Reality*, 1937). Writing in 1970, Scots poet Alan Bold, in his superlative Introduction to *The Penguin Book of Socialist Verse*, might have been writing about the mainstream poetry of the subsequent four decades:

...the contemporary poetry that gets most attention, in Britain at least, is technically inadequate, thematically limited, and socially soporific. At its best it is pleasant, at its worst pathetic. It may be that it is able to hog the spotlight because our leading critical sensibilities have so much irony in their souls they recoil from a direct and explicit mission of concern for other people. It may be that in order to consolidate the rather trivial work that they have championed they refuse to discuss art that would jeopardise this. This operation is not confined to the weekend critics. There is a rather perverse abdication of the critical faculty...

But the poetry in **Release a Rage of Red** is an emphatic riposte to such poetic complacencies. It is a further indication that political poetry is in the ascendant, as it has been since the dawn of the Tory austerity dispensation, and almost in parallel to the rise of Corbyn's authentic Labourite socialism. Both were frowned-upon, mocked as quixotic, 'unreconstructed', outdated and unfashionable, or largely ignored by the poetical and political mainstreams of the Nineties and Noughties. But now, in the more polarised Noughteens, while frowning-upon and mocking might still be attempted in some quarters, ignoring is no longer tenable.

Fortunately there exists in the UK today a thin red line of politically engaged poetry imprints that seek to publish the poetries of more 'precarious' social experience and ensure that not all impoverished, 'unemployed' or 'working-poor' poets are doomed to 'blush unseen', to quote from Thomas Gray's 'Covert Pastoral'* lament on the perennial obscurity of most working-class poets and artists, 'An Elegy Written in a Country Churchyard' (1751) (expertly deconstructed by William Empson in *Some Versions of Pastoral\**, 'I: Proletarian Literature', 1935). The prolific and long-serving Smokestack Books is one of these presses. **Culture Matters** is another and younger enterprise, and its annual Bread and Roses Poetry Award, now in its third year with this, its third publication, is specifically here to facilitate talent-scouting among working-class voices:

*Our mission is to promote a socialist approach to all cultural activities, including arts such as poetry. So we run the Bread and Roses Poetry Award to create new opportunities for working people to write poetry, and to encourage poets to focus on themes which are meaningful to working-class communities.*

What is meant here by 'working class'? Well in this day and age any conceptual Proletariat worth its salt will incorporate the more recently defined 'Precariat' (a portmanteau of 'precarious' and 'proletariat'), which cuts across the hitherto traditional lines of the authentic working class and the lower-middle class, representing all those scraping an existence in unsatisfactory and insecure employment which has been taken up through necessity rather than choice or preference. If you like, Theresa May's "Just About Managing" (JAMs), pitted against the "burning injustices" of Foodbank Britain.

In **Release a Rage of Red** we are presented with a prime sample of contemporary 'Precariat' poetry in the shape of the twenty-five highest entries —including the top five joint winners, **Jane Burn**, **Martin Hayes**, **David Hubble**, **Paul Summers** and **Rob Walton**— of the 2019 Bread & Roses Poetry Award. Here we have some highly accomplished examples of contemporary polemical poetry from a micro-canon of socially conscious poets who dextrously express and depict experiences of precarious existence.

Appropriately for the bicentenary of the Peterloo Massacre, Ruth Aylett's commemorative villanelle 'Orgreave' marks the 35th anniversary of the eponymous pitched battle during the 1984-5 Miners' Strike. Shropshire poet Gaynor Beesley's touching poem on paternal unemployment in the shadow of industrial decline, 'Cutting Back'. Sexual harassment from a male fellow supermarket worker is tackled in Jane Burn's visceral 'So, I Grabbed Ahold of My Own Cunt'. Linda Burnett on how 'We strained to extricate ourselves/ from loops of brooding drudgery without a word' in the lyrical 'A Very Northern Inheritance'. Defiant optimism on the picket line in Owen Gallagher's triumphal 'We Have Everything to Breathe For'.

Moira Garland laments library closures in the subtly rhyming 'The day libraries are outlawed'. There's Tracey Hammett's hard-hitting rap-like/ Spoken Word 'Nothing — A Protest Poem'. A definitive 'Precariat' poem in Martin Hayes' 'spines stronger than the back of the Earth'. Bernadette Horton's sharply polemical 'Working-Class Woman'. An almost surreal satirical graphite-take on 'Brexit' in David Hubble's 'Pencils'. Spirited protest in Lisa Kelly's 'This Poem has a Title'. Domestic abuse in Lisa Matthew's harrowing 'The bowl'.

Char March's 'Examining reasons for rural depopulation' begins as a seemingly tongue-in-cheek vignette but ends chillingly: 'How to never end up in the winter fields/ give birth to a rape baby in the hedge/ go straight back to digging beets'. Mexborough-based poet Ian Parks gifts a spirit-lifting poem in the Blakeian 'Trespass': 'in that forgotten lull between the wars —/the shop girls and the mill hands/ and the pit lads from the mines // ...to swarm up Jacob's Ladder and its steep stone stairs/ there was nothing they could do but give them back/ that place of light and air and rapid cloud:/ the open ground that was already theirs'.

There's also Alun Rees's satirical, nursery rhyme-like 'The History of Capitalism'. The urban biblical in Paul Summers' 'Dark'. Laura Taylor's exceptional 'Speaking in Tongues', strikingly reminiscent of Stevie Smith, depicts her experience as a working-class schoolgirl mentally rebelling against middle-class tutelage, and includes the wonderful phrase 'I heard/ that it was not for me,/ like olives and halloumi' and 'I learned/ that thought-provoking words should not be used in school,/ like primogeniture, or cultural hegemony'. Another *cri de cœur* for working-class women comes in Angela Topping's no-holds-barred 'The Bastards'.

Rob Walton's 'Bank' is a mantra-like play on foodbanks. Irish poet Alan Weadick takes us on a tour of the shop floor in an ice-cream factory where he daily sympathises with female workers subjected to managerial sexual harassment in an atmosphere of general occupational alienation: 'And we are sickened, then, us grunts/ and fork-lift jockeys of the ice cream business;/ ...the brain-freeze that silently runs whole/ ...and a lifetime's work of dreaming/ yourself elsewhere, its hands daily upon you'.

In 'Markham Main', a vignette about veterans of the Miners' Strike, Sarah Wimbush encompasses so much in just 12 lines, closing on a poignant trope: 'After school, they take the grandkids/ to the Pit Top Playground, look forward/ to the night shift at Ikea. Together'.

J. Holt Wilson's 'Plump' is a blistering polemic on the plight of immigrants and refugees, 'brought to grace/ a private space of regal greed,/ ornaments against their will/ and now considered pests,/ to be controlled', the closing verse of which culminates defiantly with the motto of Gerard Winstanley's Diggers: 'the earth's a common treasury for all'.

And finally, my own 'Phineus Among the Harpies', an allusive third-person depiction of the dispiriting and humiliating experience of being effectively put 'on trial' for one's disability at a Personal Independence Payment Tribunal Appeal Hearing.

It is an honour to be in the company of such gifted and essential poets.

*Release a Rage of Red* presents a small but powerful and important sample of contemporary poetry which is as much social document as it is poetic witness to the experiences of today's 'Precariat'.

# Contents

| | | |
|---|---|---|
| Ruth Aylett | Orgreave | 11 |
| Gaynor Beesley | Cutting Back | 12 |
| Jane Burn | So, I Grabbed Ahold of My Own Cunt | 13 |
| Linda Burnett | A Very Northern Inheritance | 15 |
| Owen Gallagher | We Have Everything to Breathe For | 17 |
| Moira Garland | The day libraries are outlawed | 18 |
| Tracey Hammett | Nothing — A Protest Poem | 19 |
| Martin Hayes | spines stronger than the back of the Earth | 21 |
| Bernadette Horton | Working-Class Woman | 23 |
| David Hubble | Pencils | 25 |
| | The Greatest Briton | 26 |
| Lisa Kelly | This Poem has a Title | 28 |
| Lisa Matthews | The bowl | 29 |
| Char March | Examining reasons for rural depopulation | 30 |
| Alan Morrison | Phineus Among the Harpies | 31 |
| Ian Parks | Trespass | 33 |
| Alun Rees | The History of Capitalism | 34 |
| Paul Summers | Dark | 36 |
| Laura Taylor | Speaking in Tongues | 38 |
| Angela Topping | The Bastards | 40 |
| Rob Walton | Bank | 42 |
| | bloke in a shed | 43 |
| Alan Weadick | Vespucci Ice Cream (The Line) | 46 |
| Sarah Wimbush | Markham Main | 48 |
| J Holt Wilson | Plump | 49 |

# Ruth Aylett

## Orgreave
*For the 35th anniversary rally, June 15 2019*

This was their lesson, a baton on the head
and the horses charging across the field,
but we became more resolute instead.

Called 'enemies within' we fell and bled
arrested, beaten, with escape routes sealed.
This was their lesson, a baton on the head.

We don't forgive the things they did and said
and don't forget the hate their lies revealed
as we become more resolute instead.

Starved back to work, the industry soon dead,
lives left to decay: nothing really healed.
This was their lesson, a baton on the head.

We'll make them pay for how they tried to tread
us down into the mud. Why should we yield?
No, we become more resolute instead.

Now millions need foodbanks to get fed
so let's fight back against the power they wield.
That was their lesson, a baton on the head,
but we became more resolute instead.

# Gaynor Beesley

## Cutting Back

When the mill stopped rolling
so did Dad.
Then he found a new job,
working our garden into clods of earth and worms.
Burrowing his spade under the cabbage tops, jimmying up spuds,
grunting like a terrier after a rat.

He gave us roses, in memoriam.
Celestial, Perpetual, Cardinal, Peace.
Their names intoned like a psalm over dinner
the salt on our vegetable stew,
the honey in our tea.

That last August I squatted on brittle earth,
feline, waiting,
as Dad bent over his bushes intent.
Sweat rimming his cap, greasing his specs,
the spiteful beak of his secateurs nipping at the stalks and heads.
The air bubbled blossoms.
He jabbed a finger, *Yoe see there Bab cut away the dead rubbish*
*'n eventually all new growth'll come through,*
and I watched until all that was left was a white bleeding stump.

# Jane Burn

## So, I Grabbed Ahold of My Own Cunt

Better that than under the thumb of the wrong man.
The one that shits a brick cos your hemline's above the knee,
the one who sights a level with your breasts.
Come, you upskirters,
    gropers,
    fiddlers.
Roll up, roll up to where we're stuck,
behind our desk, our till, our bar, our counter top, our stall.
Come,
with moisture on your smacking lips, rub keen palms
on greasy fabric thighs.
Bless us and our pursefuls of pin money, shackled
to your trouser pocket rummaging for change,
your come-to-bed conversation, leaning that bit over,
catch
a sneaky treat of tit, a clue of cleft. *Here*, you say,
as we kneel to stack a shelf. *While you're down there, pet.*
Look how we break the day around our babies,
bite our tongues
or get the boot.
Look how the bags-for-life have have swung
their weighted lacerations on our skin.
Watch us
check behind before we bend, sense you fix the open target,
thrust with the intrusion of your eyes.
Look at the glass ceiling, how we drown beneath it,
ice over a pond.

How you fear the witch that bleeds five days
and doesn't die,
how we'll only mutter on about *down below*, ask for time off
when our kids are ill. How we'll only cry.
Look how my hand closes a fist, opens like a rose.
Look how we stop going out cos we're sick
of midnight coercion whining up our legs, sniffing out the hole,
the pissed-up booze fumes tongued along our necks.
Listen to your songs — your *I know you want it,*
your justification of *blurred lines*.
I do not want the feel of you inside of me
and so I grabbed ahold of my own cunt
to save you a job,
to save me having to run.




Lyrics taken from 'Blurred Lines' sung by Robin Thicke.

# Linda Burnett

## A Very Northern Inheritance

An agony of worker aunts
passed martyrdom along the female line.
Each rivulet of steam and sweat,
reamed achingly from unsung toil,
puddled in the gene pool of the North.

Eyes halfway to heaven,
anchored by a hyphenated mouth, traced
blueprints for our own, once
old enough to wield a pan and brush
or scrub a doorstep with a donkey stone.

We strained to extricate ourselves
from loops of brooding drudgery without a word
of note or thanks, though tripped,

rimed in every far from noble pore.

We edged away, eager to shelve
the matriarchal code and frame a compact
of shared responsibility.
But, pulsing under Christmas bakes
and beautifully turned-out kids,

a vein of bitterness still sulks,
ready to suck the joy from balancing the bricks
on an impossibly stacked hod
without collapse. A niggle of rancour,
curdling the blood, leeches
the unfairness of our role.
We carry on as we were shown, destined
to bear the brunt. Unbidden
we polish off our tasks with sighs, and join
vexed martyrs on the distaff side.

# Owen Gallagher

## We Have Everything to Breathe For

Right now, workers have stopped sewing
jeans in a sweatshop in East London
and are stitching a picket line
around the factory's throat,
lighting a brazier and writing placards;
'Honk if you support a living wage!'

Beep! Beep! Beep! go the passing cars.
A purse and savings can is emptied into a hand.
A Gurdwara fires their hope with curries
and workers in McDonalds set up
a staff take-away service
to support the picket line.

As long as our eyes open there is cause to sing.
We have everything to breathe for!

# Moira Garland

## The day libraries are outlawed

We know the pompous men in dust-grey suits
*We're all in this together.*
The suits, they're in cahoots

with shiny money-making Midas touch,
a blinding mist before us grubby tribes.
Wealth is laundered by the filthy rich.

We know the tall grey building made of stone —
once filled with fairy tales, distant lands,
treasures, tyrants, risings, buried bones,

learning of those suits who'd now forbid
our gatherings and demands.
Faces, phones, to be recorded.

We know the tall grey building made of stone
its shiny plate-glass doors now caged by top-hatted
men, where riches are enthroned.

They think that they have closed our minds,
but we'll explode this shameful crime,
prime our pens, release a rage of red,
reload our libraries with words.

# Tracey Hammett

## Nothing — A Protest Poem

Nothing is coming to a place near you

Nothing is coming there's no need to form a queue

No need to care whether someone somewhere

Has a new improved, ever so slightly better nothing than you

A nothing that's sweeter or smaller and neater

A shinier nothing that's faster and sleeker.

There's no point in texting or tweeting about it

Don't ask for a selfie it just won't come out in it

No need for a loan to get into debt for it

Or end up in jail get your home repossessed for it

Or cause half the world to be poor and oppressed for it.

Some dispossessed for it

Mine all the land for it

Trawl all the seas for it

Cut down the forests and wipe out the bees for it.

Don't book in advance to avoid disappointment

There's no need for making an urgent appointment

And don't try to treat it with tablets or ointments.

It's gluten free, dairy free, vegan, organic

And you'd be surprised what it does for the planet

So claim it, it's yours

It's legal and fair

But please beware

It's just thin air.

# Martin Hayes

## spines stronger than the back of the Earth

a telephonist's mum is in our reception area demanding to speak
to a supervisor
so that she can ask him why
her daughter is in tears
and won't come out of her bedroom

the supervisor appears and asks the mum what the problem is
to which the mum asks back the same question
only fiercer

the supervisor eventually explains
that this lady's daughter
has a call count 33% below the rest of her team
and despite the counselling sessions she's been a part of
and the warnings she's received
nothing seemed to be improving
so he felt that there was nothing left for him to do
other than try and put 'a rocket up her arse'
which he did do
the afternoon before
when he came out into the telephonist room and in front of
everyone
called her a lazy good-for-nothing fucking slob
who was dragging the whole team down

the mum is enraged by this explanation
and tells the supervisor that he should be ashamed of himself

humiliating her daughter like that
in front of everyone
that if it was such a problem
then he should've pulled her into an office and told her so
professionally
like a man would
before swinging one into the side of the supervisor's head
and storming out

thus proving
once again
that you can easily break the spine
of a 16-grand-a-year 19-year-old telephonist
with gold dust in her eyes and a heart like a trumpet
but that a 56-year-old working mum of three
has a spine stronger than any man's
but especially
a supervisor's

# Bernadette Horton

## Working-Class Woman

Rich women received the vote
in 1918,
for us it was ten years later
second class,
second thoughts,
last in the game.

And there we have remained,
workhorses of each generation
iron burdens on fragile shoulders
childbearing careerists
giving way
to 21st century slavery,
of childbearing, elderly caring,
full time working shire horses.
Our shackled feet running from
menial supermarket job, to home.

The modern media ignores
Working-Class Woman.
She cannot dream of a better life
unless she wins a reality TV song contest
or marries a footballer
to be transported to
fake tans, fake eyelashes and a fake life.

Working-Class Woman
you were given the vote
but lost the right to choose the options for your life.
Working to survive, bread on the table
depends on you, often alone.
The aristo women
promised you could one day have it all,
work, children, cars,
money, exotic holidays
you were told were all in your grasp,
but so too were the realities of exhaustion, guilt, single parenting
and multiple divorce.

Only when Working-Class Woman
is represented in Parliament
by people who have walked a mile in her shoes will change in her
fortunes occur.

Until then Working-Class Woman
keep fighting like the women of old
keep shouting, keep battling
voice your struggles from the rooftops
in your communities, your union sisterhood.
For one day one from your number will
govern our country,
and finally set women and our class
free.

# Dave Hubble

## Pencils

We're taking our pencils back,
chucking out those funny foreign ones —
Staedtler, Caran d'Ache, Koh-i-Noor.
We're going it alone with graphite, sketching out
the sketchiest of plans, making our mark
'cos the scribblers have spoken,
so stockpile while the wood's still fine-grained,
before it starts to splinter and the leads
all break when you try to sharpen them,
so they'll all be a bit too short to use comfortably
because of the eternal, futile sharpening.
The other ends will all be chewed
so you feel a bit queasy about where they've been
as you absent-mindedly put them in your mouth
and taste other people's toothmarks on your tongue.
If they have rubbers,
they'll smudge rather than erase,
but most will have dropped off
just below the little ferrule
so when you try to use them,
they scratch and tear the page.
None will be coloured, just
common-or-garden common-sense
grey HB —smugglers will use any means
to flood our streets with overseas art materials
of every hue. Think about the children! Before we know it,
backstreet stationers will be selling packets of

Clutch to schoolkids, free samples of charcoal
to get the youth hooked and all
the paraphernalia —French curves, blending stumps,
stencils. Outrage! So, yes — we're taking our pencils back
and it's going to be shit.

## The Greatest Briton

We shall go on to the end,
      A lot of jolly little wars against barbarous peoples
We shall fight in France,
      conscious of a feeling of irritation that Kaffirs should be
      allowed to fire on white men
we shall fight on the seas and oceans,
hordes who [eat] little but camel dung
we shall fight with growing confidence
      The Aryan stock is bound to triumph
and growing strength in the air,
      *I am strongly in favour of using poisoned gas against*
      *uncivilized tribes*
we shall defend our island,
      [it] would spread a lively terror
whatever the cost may be.
      "Keep England White" is a good slogan
We shall fight on the beaches,
      I do not admit [...] that a great wrong has been done to the

      Red Indians of America or the Black people of Australia
we shall fight on the landing grounds,
      a stronger race, a higher-grade race [...] has come in and
      taken their place
we shall fight in the fields
      *I hate Indians. They are a beastly people with a beastly*
      *religion*
and in the streets,
      100,000 degenerate Britons should be forcibly sterilized
      and others put in labour camps.
we shall fight in the hills;
      If the striking Welsh miners are hungry we will fill their
      bellies with lead
we shall never surrender.

[*All lines are statements made by Winston Churchill, alternating with his famous wartime speech. In public polls he is consistently voted the Greatest Briton*]

# Lisa Kelly

## This Poem has a Title

This poem must take medication in order to be read
at any future event. It has been found that this poem
has an unfair natural advantage which makes it stand
out at festivals and open mic spots, and streak ahead
of its competitors. In order for the competition not to
feel demoralised, this poem must take aural contraceptives
to suppress its innate ability to propagate and inspire
other poems to try as hard as this poem. This poem
must be sterilised, and wake up lethargic and drugged,
so it becomes a non-starter and will be stripped of its title.
This poem has too many phonemes which must significantly
be reduced to sub-haiku levels. However, if this poem
refuses to subscribe to its prescription, it may be allowed
to focus on becoming a long poem of 5,000 lines
where new rules regarding the phoneme levels do not
apply. It is accepted that this ruling is discriminatory,
but is necessary, reasonable and proportionate
to ensure fair competition for all poems that are just not
as good as this poem. Any argument that this poem
should be celebrated, not regulated, will be ignored.
The future of this poem has been brought to you by
a panel despite its serious concerns about this poem
having to take frequent medication, absence of evidence
and potential harmful side-effects of phoneme treatment.
This poem has promised to fight. This poem will be heard.

# Lisa Matthews

## The bowl

As if she'd been riding side saddle and her body could not quite shake the ridiculous posture now she was back at home, she leant on the right-hand arm of the high-backed chair. Each day is a slow drag to the butcher's, the baker's; those candlestick takers running up back lanes in the dead of night, snuffing out flames with persistent fingers; we can see you, we can hear you they snide, as they insinuate themselves between coalhouse and back gate. She remembers the panic on the radio, the rush to the registrar; no one told her about the bargains she'd have to make, the blind eyes she'd have to fake, wincing as she adjusts the dial. How she considers the stain blooming across the cornice as he seethes away, night after night, on top of her. There were times when she flew out of the door and across the city, past the river to where no one else would ever have to squat over a bowl of bleach on the scullery floor. What sort of man brings that home, what sort of man stays after that? The shame of it all falling across the front of the house like the shadow from the barrage. At least she had the children first, because they wouldn't happen now. Not after this. She wipes the bowl, leans it against the taps, he folds the paper on the table and winds his watch.

# Char March

## Examining reasons for rural depopulation

My grandma taught me how to carry trays
How to position all the spouts —teapot, coffeepot, cream jug—
pointing away from me on the leading edge of the tray
How to open a heavy door while carrying a tray
How to gather spent glasses in the careful dance
that never allowed his lordship
between me and the door
How to avoid the footman, the stable hand, the butler, the delivery boy
How to starch my cap so I could see clear to edges of Lincolnshire
How to never end up in the winter fields
give birth to a rape baby in the hedge
go straight back to digging beets

# Alan Morrison

## Phineus Among the Harpies

The appeal was refused by the tribunal, the tribunal numbered
Three: an insouciant judge, a glacial lawyer, and a GP
Who wilfully misinterpreted him, pinned him at cross-purposes,
Kept making a point of his insight and articulacy —
Qualities going against his case, as if to imply the mentally
Afflicted must be stupid, when it's almost always the opposite case,
Her assumption that intelligence bestows prolific phrenic
Equipment to cope with any symptom of mind, even
The *ego-dystonic*, a term he'd picked up from some foxed
Blue-spined Pelican (pain makes its own experts), attempting
To explain the impetus of Pure Obsessional Disorder:
That it matters not one whit whether he would act on his
Intrusive thoughts, present risk, this bore no relevance
To the intensity of distress, the inexorable anxiety
Rooted in uncertainty, ever-mutating *symptomatology*,
A mind besieged by obsessions*; something about him caused
Them umbrage, the three 'impartial' panel members, apparently
'Independent' from Independent Assessment Services
(Atos formerly), and the DWP; pernickety Harpies
Handpicked for nitpicking pedantry, pecking at the scraps of his
Incapacity —he, hapless Phineus, half-crippled by phobias;
Supposed experts deciding his entitlement, or not,
To Personal Independence Payment (PIP (excuse the ellipses));
They even used his avoidance behaviours to argue that he was
High-functioning in spite of therapists' emphases that these
Repetitious rituals are symptoms not coping mechanisms
That retard healing of psychical scars; he might have quoted

Kierkegaard, something along the lines that all the torments
Of the damned pale in comparison to anxiety: excoriating
Guilt of the innocent, gut-aching angst in the absence of an act
(Hamletic hesitation), spent nerves of no event, but that
Would have also gone against him —as it did that he went
To university, and, more intrusively, that creative writing
Was his *'hobby'* (how suburban that sounded!) which makes him
Probably a bit bohemian, thus unreliable, rebellious, anti-
Establishment, and while he might convince as an idiot savant,
He'd obviously been embroidering the truth to a more threadbare
                brocade
When claiming he was number-blind, they pointed out he'd
Have had to tackle statistics while studying Sociology —
Not as far as he could recall, but in any case he'd later changed
To Ancient History... At school it took until he was fourteen
To see what the clock face had so long been trying to tell him,
A lightning-struck Damascene of horology! Now Old Chronos
Could no longer cock a snook —a little death erupted in him then,
A peripheral epiphany, still trapped in fight or flight of tick-
Tock neuroticism permanently ruminating on past and future,
Never mentally in the present, temporally absent, but at last
Able to tell the time without having to guess, now everything
Pressed more urgently, reassurance at least in grasping
That suffering was time-limited as contribution-based benefits...

\*This is a tautology: the Latin root *obsessus* means *besieged*.
\*\* From the Latin: *angere*: *to choke*.

# Ian Parks

## Trespass

It takes just one gamekeeper and his gun
to scare a pair of walkers from the land.
It takes a pack of growling dogs
to stop them in their tracks, to see them off

and send them back the way the came.
It only takes a crude, hand-pained sign
to keep the Sunday ramblers at bay.
But when they met in thousands as they did

in that forgotten lull between the wars —
the shop girls and the mill hands
and the pit lads from the mines —
the unexpected morning when they came

to swarm up Jacob's Ladder and its steep stone stairs
there was nothing they could do but give them back
that place of light and air and rapid cloud:
the open ground that was already theirs.

# Alun Rees

## The History of Capitalism

Time was when life was bad as bad
and crap and tripe and trash.
Then chaps who yearned for progress
one day invented cash.

But somehow things got worse and worse
and worse and worse and worse
and worser yet until they were
the worsest of the worst.

In time they went from worst to foul,
to vile and then obscene,
and from obscene to grimmest yet,
the worst they'd ever been.

Yet still life went from there to worse
and viler yet and viler
and worse than that and worse again
and fouler still and fouler.

Up the big house the rich men sat,
a gross eternal curse,
and things got worse and worse and worse
and worser and more worse.

When the rich looked down they said the poor
were quite beyond the pale,
and just for laughs they'd jack the price
of food and fags and ale.

And all the poor could do was rage
and wave each empty purse
while the fat and rich grew fatter yet
and worse and worse and worse.

# Paul Summers

## Dark

*In den finsteren Zeiten,*
*wird da auch gesungen werden?*
*Da wird auch gesungen werden.*
*Von den finsteren Zeiten.*
—Bertolt Brecht

& on the eighth day
there was darkness
again. even darker
than the last time
but not a patch on
the next if you believe
that weird, little god-nik
fucker at the monument.
darker than that time
you gaffer taped my eyes.
darker than that night
we hammered the poitín
in davy's da's shed & you
bit off the ears of his sister's
classroom gerbil. darker
than the entire contents
of johnny cash's wardrobe.
darker than the core of an
overlooked verruca. dark
as fuck, apart from a pulse
of weak, pale light emitted

in the west from the burnt-
out convoy of overturned
police-vans currently blocking
all six lanes of the A1(M) in both
directions, & from jimmy upstairs,
who has somehow rigged an old
black & white portable to a car-
battery so he can watch **attheraces**
completely unimpeded by events
of global significance, & your
slightly eccentric, europhile
neighbour; the one with the nice
job & the buy-to-let mortgage,
engaged in an act of quiet
immolation there in the back-lane,
precariously close to our wheelie-bin.
apart from all that though, it's dark
as fuck. much darker than the last time,
not a patch on the next.

# Laura Taylor

## Speaking in Tongues

They said
*too clever for your own good.*

I heard
that it was not for me,
like olives and halloumi

and
*must you question everything?*
Unintended irony.

They own
the land and property.

I face
reduced mortality.

*The politics of envy*
is for the likes of me.

The politics of greed
are what I clearly see.

I learned
that thought-provoking words should not be used in school,
like primogeniture, or cultural hegemony.

They said
*what do you want to be?*
*A nurse or secretary?*

Then
*tell me what the poem means.*

I said that it was not for me.
Refused. Would not reduce.

*There is one meaning, learn it well*
*so you can pass your O level.*

I didn't.

Instead
I tore my tongue in two,
threw salt across a wall of eyes,
soaked my throat in dissonance
and didn't
listen to their lies.
I saw that all the world's for me,
that they could keep dishonesty,
and laughed,
eating olives and halloumi.

# Angela Topping

## The Bastards

They tried to stop me by saying I was too young and ignorant
They tried to stop me with you're too old
They tried to stop me by saying I was at that age
They tried to stop me by giving me too much homework
They tried to stop me because I was doing it all wrong
They tried to stop me by asking me to make all the beds
They tried to stop me by saying people like me couldn't
They tried to stop me by letting me then stopping me
They tried to stop me by hanging me upside down by my toes
They tried to stop me by making me watch Disney films until
    I was sick
They tried to stop me by forcing me outside and saying I didn't
    live there now
They tried to stop me by giving me dolly mixtures and Smarties
They tried to stop me by changing my name
They tried to stop me by locking me out of the library
They tried to stop me by pretending to show me how
They tried to stop me with go on then show us how it's done
They tried to stop me by unravelling my knitting and giving
    the yarn to Oxfam
They tried to stop me by exorcising the house
They tried to stop me by giving me praise for doing what they
    wanted
They tried to stop me by tracing a finger on my mantelpiece and
    showing me the dirt
They tried to stop me by sending me to the shop on a message
They tried to stop me by going la la la when I talked

They tried to stop me by burying me in a pit and saying I was a
    bear
They tried to stop me until they ran out of ideas and held a
    meeting
They tried to stop me by dropping me down the agenda
    but only half way down so I would know my place
They tried to stop me by binding me with silver, driving a stake
    through my heart


First published on *The Fat Damsel*

# Rob Walton

## Bank

Write poems on the tins you put in the foodbank
Write verse about how foodbank even became a word
Write about alternatives to foodbanks
Write long lines about love conquering all
Write about love not necessarily being a short-term
solution for the starving
Write that then again maybe love is the answer
Write about protest and togetherness
Write advice about where to get better advice
Write the ingredients for a revolution on a packet
of something indulgent
Write about the need for treats
Write about the need for levity and seriousness
Write about us and them
Write about whether there is ultimately only us
Write about rights and responsibilities
Write about ending austerity and words of plenty
Write about writing a Closed sign on the last foodbank.

## bloke in a shed

there's a bloke in a shed
let's call him david, for argument's sake

he's pushing his hand through his hair, his lovely hair
he's writing in his shed, his lovely shed

writing about this time, this golden olden time
this time, a couple of years ago

when he invited, *sod it, let's just do it*
he wanted to leave his mark, his lovely mark,

when he invited this other bloke, let's call him goliath,
for the sake of an argument — a good old fairly-fought ding-dong

he invited him to his wife's stately home for the weekend
said they should work together, they were on the same side

they were above petty squabbles
and petty squabblers and philistines, whatever they were

and this david and this so-called goliath laughed together
mind, how they laughed

and they talked of taking pot-shots
even though they knew this other bloke

who, for the sake of a bit of peace and quiet, we'll now call boris
they knew him as the real pot-shot man

and back then they decided scattershots were a blast
you could hit targets you didn't even know were targets

as long as you were behind the gun you were safe
as long as you were behind the gun you were laughing

and some other lovely folk in this lovely country
were ooh beside themselves with something

on a lovely family outing to a lovely stately home
and they saw these two blokes in an upstairs window

having a proper laugh without a care, without a care
polishing the shotguns and other weaponry

*you don't need licences round here*
*no-one checks that sort of stuff round here*

*they're that busy hiring or is it firing Poles*
*and treading and not treading on battery hens*

they started to take aim at lombardy poplar
and scots pine and norwegian spruce

and *cedars of bleedin' lebanon*
and something david swore was *blasted turkey bastard oak*

next up they aimed at the visitors who arrived on a dirty red bus
wearing laughable cagoules and the wrong hoodies

*they didn't get those from Cornwall!*
*that's not organic cotton!*

*if you can't see its face give it both barrels*
*just to be on the safe side*

it was all pretty indiscriminate to tell a sort of truth
the shooting of petty squabblers and moaning minnies

and hearts of oak and babes in arms
and hit or miss they howled just the same

and raised hip flasks with crude engravings
as boris/goliath asked *what's next and where do we go from here*

*well dinner is at eight and george is bringing pie face*
*and he keeps writing things about me and him*
*and shooting and chances and saloons but sod it*
*it won't be as good as my lovely writing in my lovely shed*
*what I will do when it's all blown over*
*and he's still bringing pie face and shiraz is thicker than water*
*thicker than la manche and these people out there*
*are thicker than anything*
*and christ I'm thirsty*
*I need a lovely drink*
*ring the bloody bell*
*that bloody division bell*
*why don't you*
*ring the bloody bell*

# Alan Weadick

## Vespucci Ice Cream (The Line)

On a dream-slick floor I trudge between
the humming, churning vats and *The Line*
where a dozen white linen and plastic-capped women
milk tub after tub of the on- tap gold
streaming from silver faucets
hour after hour, till they run dry after dark.

Days I toss boxes in and out of freezer trucks,
see a brave new world of previously unheard-of
seaside towns from a smoke-filled transit cab, collect
a surprising amount of nods, winks and advances
from around posh supermarket *Goods In* entrances.
But it all comes back to the factory floor
with a longing I see mirrored in the drivers' and helpers' faces
as we all drift back there near close of business
to gaze at the women on *The Line*.

Made anything but shapeless in their overalls
they sway a beat or two behind the rhythm of excess,
taming the spiralling swirls of vanilla, raspberry-ripple,
chocolate and banana, gushing in unceasing surfeit;
such grace under the pressure of an unstoppable clock
is something you see every day
but can somehow never get enough of.

Unless it's erased, by the sudden whim of a boss,
a roving manager, or one of the owners, some emperor
of everything, stepping up behind that day's candidate,
one of that line under orders not to waste a drop.
Holding her helpless in his arms,
hands busily out of our sight,
he nuzzles her stiffened neck
or nibbles the lobe of her ear,
with his hips clamped on to hers,
constricting her already tiny orbit —
in that space where you can't hear yourself speak
for the precision-timed grind of noise —
till his moment's hunger is gratified.

And we are sickened, then, us grunts
and fork-lift jockeys of the ice cream business;
queasy with a mouthful of outrage, a splutter of envy
and a few other mystery ingredients
you wouldn't have thought would go together,
but do, every day, like the taste of ice-cream,
the brain-freeze that silently runs whole
glittering universes of work
and a lifetime's work of dreaming
yourself elsewhere, its hands daily upon you.

# Sarah Wimbush

## Markham Main

Afternoons, they meet up
on street corners
like old youths planning revolution.

Gaffers, fathers, brothers —
an hour at the Club with a pint.
Go over the end again, and again.

How they were the last by three days
to stay out in Yorkshire.
How they'd *gu back tomorra*.

After school, they take the grandkids
to the Pit Top Playground, look forward
to the night shift at Ikea. Together.

# J Holt Wilson

## Plump

Amassed atop an autumn lake
in hush and dusk, a brown-backed flush
of silent migrants gather.
No passport checks, no border guards.
They wait, prepare to feather air
to Beauly Firth, to fertile ground, to safety
in formation.

We stop to watch the tea-time mob,
pass comment on the novelty.
Remember they were brought to grace
a private space of regal greed,
ornaments against their will
and now considered pests,
to be controlled.

Fickle England pricks the eggs
of babies loathed before they're born.
Their problem is they made themselves
too comfortably at home;
it doesn't matter where they roam,
they'll always be pariahs,
never celebrated travellers
on pedestals.

A chorus of chaotic honks signals their departure.
We watch them breaking through the trees,
a genius of vortices, untrammelled
and behove to no authority.
Unravelling in bright-eyed glee,
we laugh in solidarity;
the earth's a common treasury for all.

\* The collective noun for a group of geese on the ground is a gaggle; when in flight, they are called a skein, a team, or a wedge; when flying close together, they are called a plump.

Recent publications from **Culture Matters**, available from http://www.culturematters.org.uk/index.php/shop-support/our-publications

### **Robots Have No Bones** by Fred Voss (2019)

In a series of sympathetic, sometimes visionary poems, **Voss** takes us into the lives of the American working class, manual workers who have been betrayed by successive politicians. Technological advances like robots mean that there is enough wealth being created for working people not to have to work so hard, for so long, and for so little — but capitalism makes that impossible.

### *Shabbigentile* by Alan Morrison (2019)

A counterpoint to his Forward Prize -nominated **Tan Raptures** (Smokestack Books, 2017), Alan Morrison's ***Shabbigentile*** depicts an asset-stripped Britain where red top propaganda against the unemployed and disabled is a scapegoating pseudo-science (Scroungerology) recycling eugenicist rhetoric; and the DWP's weapons of brown envelopes are transmuted into Salted Caramels. The potentially catastrophic cross-paths of 'Brexit', Trump and insurgent European-wide right-wing populism are also poetically confronted.

### **One of These Dead Places** by Jane Burn (2018)

One of the voices rarely heard in modern poetry is that of working-class women, in terms of both the impact of major historical events on their identity, health and happiness, as well as their day-to-day experiences of work, men and motherhood. In this remarkable, powerful collection, Jane Burn has told her story and more, in a series of poems which are both personal and political. She has also illustrated the poems with a beautifully imaginative series of illustrations, which add depth and detail to the collection.

### We Will Be Free! The Bread and Roses Poetry Award Anthology 2018
edited by Mike Quille, with an Introduction by Len McCluskey (2018)

The anthology of poems from the 2018 poetry award, sponsored by Unite.

### From Aberfan t Grenfell by Mike Jenkins and Alan Perry (2018)

**From Aberfan t Grenfell** shows that Mike Jenkins's sublime skills in dialect poetry continue to shine as brightly as ever, as he evokes a bravura array of voices from his Merthyr bro. Using his work to give speech to people without power, Jenkins's poetry dramatizes the characters and struggles of a community —but also a community's surviving capacity to raise its voices against the power-structures which cause it to suffer. Compassionate and incisive in equal measure, **From Aberfan t Grenfell** is required reading in an era of austerity. Superbly illuminated by Alan Perry's artwork, this book shows that, in Mike Jenkins' hands, poetry is not only an unflinching mirror but also a righteous hammer.

### The Trouble with Monsters by Christopher Norris (2018)

This new collection of political poems take aim at some monsters of our present bad times, among them Donald Trump, Boris Johnson, Jacob Rees-Mogg, Theresa May, George Osborne, Benjamin Netanyahu, and assorted hangers-on. They are held to account here in verse-forms that are tight and sharply focused despite the intense pressure of feeling behind them. The satire is unsparing and the dominant tone is one of anger mixed with sorrow, and a vivid sense of the evils and suffering brought about by corruptions of political office.

### Ruses and Fuses by Fran Lock, with images by Steev Burgess (2018)

The follow-up book to **Muses and Bruises** (see below). In this collection, Fran takes us to the rebellious, inspiring heart of English dissent with her portrayals of Levellers and Diggers such as Gerard Winstanley and Ned Ludd, and their fight with authorities over property rights. As with her first collection, **Ruses and Fuses** is adorned with the wonderful collages of Steev Burgess. Together they rail powerfully against today's right- wing global threat to the livelihoods of working-class people.

**Power Play** by Mair De-Gare Pitt with images by Jill Powell (2018)

From the very first poem this collection focuses on the human and, through its brilliant lyricism, elevates the experiences it describes into something like beauty. The collection understands that the real way to political change is by moving people, by getting hold of their hearts, and by writing memorably, which the poems do again and again. There are some beautiful accompanying paintings by Jill Powell, which widen and deepen the meanings of the poems.

**Poetry on the Picket Line: an anthology** edited by Grim Chip and Mike Quille, with an Introduction by Phill Jupitus (2018)

This anthology of poems is sponsored by PCS, RMT and the TUC (London, East and South East Region). **Poetry on the Picket Line** is a squad of writers prepared to turn up on picket lines and read poetry. Something a bit different, and it usually goes down well. The poets do what it says on the tin. They turn up at pickets and demos and read poems — with a mic, without a mic, through a bullhorn, whatever. Pickets are generally pretty pleased and surprised to see them. They appreciate the support, and some of them even appreciate the poetry!

*Poetry with principles. Poetry with a point. Poetry on the picket line. That's where it should be* —Billy Bragg

**arise!** by Paul Summers (2018)

This pamphlet-length poem is sponsored by Durham Miners' Association and introduced by its Secretary, Alan Cummings. It celebrates the rich heritage and culture of mining communities, and the collective and co-operative spirit of past generations of men and women who worked and struggled so hard to survive, to build their union, and to organise politically to fight for a better world. The poem also celebrates the new, resurgent spirit in the Labour Party, and the renewal of support for socialist solutions to the country's growing economic and social problems.

*It's wonderful to see the proud history of the Durham Miners' Gala represented in this powerful poem. Paul Summers has managed to capture the spirit of the Miners' Gala and its central place in our movement's mission to achieve 'victory for the many, and not the few'* —Jeremy Corbyn

### The Combination by Peter Raynard (2018)

Peter Raynard has written a remarkable new long poem to mark the 200th anniversary of Marx's birth, and the 170th anniversary of the publication of the Communist Manifesto. Like the Manifesto, it protests the injustice and exploitation which is integral to capitalism, and the growing gap between capitalism's productive potential and the unequal distribution of its benefits. And like that Manifesto, it is a dynamic and powerful piece of writing — pungent, oppositional and unsettling.

### The Things Our Hands Once Stood For by Martin Hayes (2018)

Martin Hayes is the only British poet who writes consistently and seriously about work, and about the insanity of a society where employees are seen merely as mere 'hands' to be employed and to make money for their employer. The clear message of his poetry is that those who do the work should own, control, and benefit fully from it.

### A Third Colour by Alan Dunnett and Alix Emery (2018)

Through the sheen of vivid, simple narratives and vignettes in this book, we glimpse more disturbing, ambivalent themes of alienation, dislocation and suffering, the psychological fallout of anxiety in modern capitalist culture. **A Third Colour** is a book of visionary, poetic parables and dystopian, uneasy images. It is a principled and skilful expression of —and protest against— the world we live in.

### Muses and Bruises by Fran Lock with images by Steev Burgess (2017)

Fran Lock's feminist and socialist poetry weaves psychological insight and social awareness into themes of poverty, mental health problems, sexual abuse, domestic violence and political struggle. It is vivid, lavish and punchy, combining a deep sense of anger and injustice with vulnerable empathy and compassion. The fragmented yet coherent collages of Steev Burgess complement and enhance those meanings perfectly. His images dance with the poems, singing together about muses and bruises, fantasy and reality — grind and grime with a lick of glitter.

### The Mouse and the Milk by Mike Quille and John Gordon (2017)

This illustrated children's book is a new version of a classic folk-tale from Sardinia, written down in 1931 by Antonio Gramsci, the Marxist philosopher and political activist, in a letter to his children. The story was later re-told by John Berger.

### Bring The Rising Home!
### by Mike Jenkins with images by Gustavius Payne (2017)

A collection of poems and images with themes of individual isolation and alienation, expressing the urgent need to recognize that collective action is necessary to change the conditions of working people. Mike Jenkins's vivid, lyrical poems work together with Gustavius Payne's bold, striking, and deeply sympathetic paintings, complementing each other perfectly.

### The Earth and the Stars in the Palm of Our Hand by Fred Voss (2017)

Fred Voss has been a metalworker in workshops in Long Beach, California for over 30 years. His poems are set in the world of work — the workers and bosses in the machine shop where he works, the social usefulness of the products they make, the alienation, aggression and camaraderie of the workplace and the relationship of work to the wider world. The poems criticise that world, but also envision a better, fairer world, in and out of the workplace.

### Lugalbanda — Lover of the Seed by Doug Nicholls (2017)

Produced as a fundraiser for the Free Ocalan campaign, this new version of a 5,000 year old poem speaks out afresh to our times, with lyrical skill and political relevance.

### On Fighting On! The Bread and Roses Poetry Anthology 2017

An anthology of poems from the Bread and Roses Poetry Award 2017, sponsored by Unite. Edited by Mike Quille, with an Introduction by Len McCluskey.

**Slave Songs and Symphonies** by David Betteridge and Bob Starrett (2017)

**Slave Songs and Symphonies** is an ambitious, beautifully crafted collection of poems, images and epigraphs. It's about human history, progressive art and music, campaigns for political freedom, social justice and peace. Above all it's about the class and cultural struggle of workers 'by hand and by brain' to regain control and ownership of the fruits of their labour.

**The Minister for Poetry Has Decreed** by Kevin Higgins (2017)

**The Minister for Poetry Has Decreed** is political poetry of the highest order, telling truth to power and poking fun at it at the same time, artistically deploying a profoundly moral sense of justice and truth to expose lies, evasions, greed and sheer stupidity.

See **www.culturematters.org.uk** for full details of our current publications.